Nothing too small

❖

Are not two sparrows sold for a penny? Yet not one of them will fall to the ground outside your Father's care. And even the very hairs of your head are all numbered. So don't be afraid; you are worth more than many sparrows.

Matthew 10:29–31

On holiday in the Lake District we went to the parish church on Sunday morning. As we walked in, we were handed a sheet of notices, along with the hymn book. Sitting in the quiet before the service began, I read through the notices. They were mainly details of the coming week's events, but at the bottom of the page was a short list of items for prayer.

I read them. First came 'Pray for world leaders talking about nuclear disarmament.' Next, 'Pray for Maggie Smith and her housing problem.'

I smiled to myself. It seemed a bit incongruous. First, the subject of earth-shattering nuclear weapons, and their control. And, next to it, Maggie Smith and her house. It was important to her, I was sure, but it was a small local problem that would never hit the headlines.

On second thoughts though, it wasn't incongruous at all. That's what God is like. He's concerned about every aspect of life, everyone's life. Yours and mine. God tells the prophet Haggai, "I will shake the nations..." (Haggai 2:7). And Jesus assures us, "Not a sparrow will fall to the ground apart from the will of your Father." And that's all the same God.

Nothing too large for him, nothing too small. He's as concerned about my small problems and needs as he is about the great political issues. As concerned about my future as about the world's.

Whatever concerns us today, he's there with us, lovingly involved, and we can take comfort.

Lord of the great, it's difficult to understand quite how, but all the world's concerns that scare me so, are somehow in your hands. And taking that to heart, I find my courage a little greater than it was before.

Extract from Facing the Storm, *first published* 1989.

Autumn in the Lake District

The princess and the frog

"But a Samaritan, as he travelled, came where the man was;
and when he saw him, he took pity on him."
Luke 10:33

A beautiful princess was walking through the palace garden with her sister when they saw a frog. The frog spoke. "I'm not really a frog," he said. "I've been bewitched and if you'll pick me up and kiss me I'll turn back into a handsome prince. We'll fall in love and live happily ever after." The princess picked up the frog, looked at him and then put him in her handbag. "Why don't you kiss him?" asked her sister. "Oh, said the princess. "There's a handsome prince on every street corner but with a talking frog I can make a fortune."

Love or money. Compassion or market forces? Which do we value most? A report on TV told of a couple who were running a successful business but they were giving all their profits away to help other people. One of them said, "We believe you become a millionaire when you've given a million pounds away, not when you've got a million pounds in the bank." I think that's great.

Of course most of us would like the chance of choosing what to do with our first million, but the principle's good. What do we do with what we've got, whether it's money in the bank or our talents and abilities? We can use what we have for ourselves or we can use it to give something to the community we live in. It's great to hear of people who put others first in such a positive and practical way as that business couple.

A Walk in the Park

Really successful living can be counted by the folk we've helped along the way rather than by what we've squirrelled away for ourselves.

Lord, giver of life and love, may I share as much in giving as in getting.

Extract from Love is a Wild Bird, *first published* 2003.

Town ducks and country ducks

❖

Accept one another, then, just as Christ accepted you,
in order to bring praise to God.
Romans 15:7

Someone's discovered that ducks in south-east London quack differently from ducks born and bred in Cornwall. Honestly. Ducks have regional accents! The reason seems to be that London ducks become more strident by having to compete with the sounds of heavy traffic and other noise pollution. Cornish ducks quack more gently. It's quieter in Cornwall, except on Bank holidays. But in the end a duck is a duck right down to the last tail feather, however refined its accent. They all have similar needs – for food and water, especially water, a safe nest, and a sense of belonging.

It sets my imagination going a bit though. What would happen if a well-brought-up Cornish duck took a London drake home to meet her parents? What would they say? "Yes, he's a nice enough bird, but I hope you're not going to marry him."

Maybe that suggests something about us human beings. Whatever our background, our accent, or even what language we speak, God made us human, with similar needs, especially the need to belong, to be accepted. Under the skin, or in the ducks' case under the feathers, we're all the same. The little differences just make life a bit more interesting.

*Lord of diversity, I thank you for the differences that shape our lives.
And for loving me for what I am.*

Extract from Chasing the Leaves, *first published* 2003.

An Afternoon Meeting

When life falls in...

Listen to my words, LORD, consider my lament.
Hear my cry for help, my King and my God, for to you I pray.
Psalm 5:1–2

I was hit by a shower of toilet rolls this morning. Fortunately not the brand that has the puppy attached. Just ordinary toilet rolls. We buy them 16 at a time – toilet rolls, not puppies – because they're cheaper that way and there's no telling when emergencies happen, which is why they're called emergencies I suppose.

Storm Clouds over Northumberland

We store the rolls in a wall cupboard above the doors of the fitted wardrobe in our bedroom. But when I slid open the wardrobe door looking for a clean shirt, down came the toilet tissue on my head.

"Stuff happens," as the American politician said, most of it a lot more difficult to cope with than that, and we can't really prepare ourselves for it. My immediate reaction when something unpleasant happens is to ask, "Why me?" Sometimes there is a reason. In this case I was in a hurry and just threw the rolls into the cupboard without checking whether they were safe or not, and so, later on, down they came.

But more often we can't identify a reason, and there's no point in looking for one. You just pick up the loo rolls, or whatever it was that hit you, and try to find the strength to carry on. And usually, if we've sown the seeds of friendship beforehand, we'll find there's someone who will help us pick up the fallen debris.

Lord, when life falls down on us,
thank you for the friends who help me pick up the pieces.

Extract from Dabbling with Ducks, *first published* 2007.

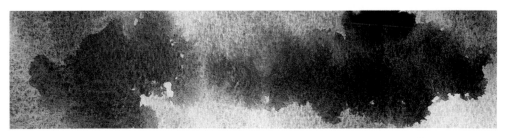

Harness your imagination

❖

Do not forget to show hospitality to strangers, for by so doing some people have shown hospitality to angels without knowing it.
Hebrews 13:2

Georgia is one of our granddaughters. One day when she was about five years old the family was in the car and playing 'I spy'. It was Georgia's turn. She said, "I spy with my little eye something beginning with c." Everyone looked around. "Car," shouted one. "Cushion." "Carpet." "Clutch." It was none of those.

Finally everyone gave up. "Crisps," said Georgia triumphantly.

"We can't see crisps," someone said. "You're only supposed to choose things you can see."

"I can see them," Georgia answered.

"Where?"

"In my mind."

"We can't see them there," said the others.

"Well you could if you tried," said Georgia, emphatically. End of discussion.

Imagination is one of God's greatest gifts. I'm not talking about thinking up a convincing reason for being late for work, but the gift of seeing things in a way others don't. The ability to put ourselves into other people's lives.

Norfolk

If we could use our imagination a bit more, and feel what it must be like to be forced from home by fear or violence, or because there just isn't enough food for the family, then we might be a fraction more welcoming and a little less critical of the strangers in our midst.

> *Lord, let me see the world through your eyes,*
> *and keep me sensitive to others' needs.*

Extract from Love is a Wild Bird, *first published* 2003.

Think twice before you bark

❖

But the fruit of the Spirit is love, joy, peace, forbearance, kindness, goodness, faithfulness, gentleness and self-control. Against such things there is no law.
Galatians 5:22–23

Did you know that dogs like watching television? Well, Milli, our new puppy, certainly does. Yes, she really does. She's not very selective and can't use the remote control yet, but she knows what she likes. Rather, she knows what she doesn't like. She doesn't like other dogs on the box. The moment she sees one, or hears one bark, she's there, growling at the screen. She doesn't realise the dogs aren't real – just virtual images as we say – she barks anyway.

We used to have a dog who disliked opera singers, particularly tenors. Whether it was Placido Domingo or Pavarotti or Carreras, it was all the same to him. When he heard them sing, he sat in front of the telly, head in the air, and howled.

But back to Milli. It's not only dogs. Anything large that moves quickly across the screen disturbs her. She just doesn't understand that the threat isn't real, there's no danger. I know people like Milli. People who feel threatened by anything or anyone new or different. And whatever they don't understand they do the human equivalent of barking at it. Even if there's no real threat.

But if I look honestly at myself, I'll find I sometimes do the same. But it's better to be positive, to welcome the new and the different, and to think twice before we bark. Or even learn not to bark at all. That's our next job in training Milli.

You ask a lot, Lord. Where shall I start?
Maybe with patience – I guess that's where you have to start with me.

Extract from Chasing the Leaves, *first published* 2003.

Milli

Something for nothing

"Freely you have received, freely give."
Matthew 10:8

Time to renew my motor insurance. Same time every year. Do I look for a new insurer, or stick with the old? Everyone seems to want my business. Adverts everywhere saying, "We're cheaper than the others. Save money with us."

I had this idea. If I went to an insurer who said he was cheaper and got a quote, I could mention that to the next insurer and get one cheaper still. Then on to the next and, if I worked at it, I'd get insurance cover for nothing. And, in my deepest fantasy, someone might even pay me for joining them.

The trouble is it doesn't happen like that. Something for nothing never works out that way. Not just in motor insurance but in relationships too. Relationships cost. They cost in commitment; we can change our motor insurance every year but if we try that in our relationships we're soon in trouble. They cost in effort too. In caring for the other person. It doesn't come cheap but in our relationships the more we give the more we get in return, although that's not why we do it. It's all about that four-letter word: love.

Generous Lord, nothing comes for nothing, except your love.
Thank you.

Extract from Chasing the Leaves, *first published* 2003.

April Wind

19

A splash of colour

❖

"See how the flowers of the field grow. They do not labour or spin. Yet I tell you that not even Solomon in all his splendour was dressed like one of these. If that is how God clothes the grass of the field, which is here today and tomorrow is thrown into the fire, will he not much more clothe you – you of little faith."
Matthew 6:28–30

Another cold winter morning, and not many smiles about. I walked through the echoing concrete tunnel under the road from the car park. Halfway down there was a door. 'Emergency Exit' it said and, underneath, 'This Door Is Alarmed'. "Well, me too," I thought, alone and with no-one else in sight. But then, as I emerged safely into the light at the other end of the tunnel, the first thing I saw was a flower stall. The flowers were gorgeous, bucketfuls of colour, a whole live rainbow just standing there to lift my spirits.

It may have been a struggle to grow them, although they've probably been reared under acres of heated glass in Holland or flown in from Kenya, but they were singing a song without words. A song about the beauty of life and creation.

It's so easy in these dark, dull days to concentrate on the negative – and some folk honestly can't help it and deserve our sympathy – but as I walk around with my own problems, I try to catch a bit of that colour and beauty, most of it unexpected, that adds a little cheer to the day. Thank God for it.

Gracious Lord, your presence colours my life with joy;
and when clouds gather help me hold your beauty close.

Extract from Dabbling with Ducks, *first published* 2007.

Flowers on the Patio

Running time backwards

❖

Do not condemn and you will not be condemned.
Forgive and you will be forgiven.
Luke 6:37

Our youngest granddaughter, Georgia, is now six-going-on-25. Talking to Mummy the other day, Georgia asked, "Mum, can we run time backwards?" What a question from a six-year-old. Mum probed a bit. No, Georgia hadn't been watching sci-fi films on telly. She'd been with a group of school friends sharing sweets, and Georgia had missed out. There hadn't been enough to go round. She thought if she could go back in time and live that bit over again, she could make sure she got a sweet.

Running time backwards. I guess we'd all like to do that at some time in our lives. To savour some happy moment, or to get a chance to put right something we regretted. "If only I had my time over again, I'd do that differently," we say.

The trouble is we can't turn the clock back, or run time in reverse. We simply – or not so simply – have to try to get it right first time. That's not always possible – I know that well from my own experience – but there can be comfort in looking honestly at mistakes we've made, facing the consequences and saying sorry. And when it's the other way round and someone's upset us, comfort in forgiving them.

And if we could run time backwards and get another chance, who's to say we'd get it right the second time round?

Forgiving Lord, I offer you my failures and regrets.
Knowing that I've tried my best must be enough for me right now.

Extract from Chasing the Leaves, *first published* 2003.

Chasing the Gulls

23

Cutting problems down to size

As the Philistine moved closer to attack him, David ran quickly towards the battle
line to meet him. Reaching into his bag and taking out a stone,
he slung it and struck the Philistine on the forehead. The stone sank into
his forehead, and he fell face down on the ground.
So David triumphed over the Philistine with a sling and a stone...
1 Samuel 17:48–50

Do you remember the story of David and Goliath? Goliath's the baddy, a giant soldier stronger than anyone else. David's a shepherd boy, the young hero who, with great courage and faith in his God, went out with a sling and hit the giant in the forehead with a stone. Exit giant, minus head.

I used to find that story a bit hard to believe. Killing a strong man with a small stone seemed unlikely. Then I visited the British Museum in London. They've got sling stones there that were dug up in Israel by archaeologists. They're as big as cricket balls – the stones, not the archaeologists – and thrown expertly by a sling can travel at a hundred miles an hour. That could change the face of cricket. It certainly changed the face of Goliath.

The Bible tells us that when David first saw Goliath, David was up on a hillside, Goliath in the valley below. My guess is that from up there the giant didn't look so big. But as David moved down and nearer, the giant seemed to get bigger and bigger, more threatening.

That's how our problems sometimes appear. The nearer they get, the bigger and heavier we feel they are, but they're the same size really.

Someone imagined David's reaction as he saw the giant close up. His first thought was, "He's big!" but his next thought was, "I can't miss!"

Some of our problems are only as big as we make them and can be cut down to size with a bit of courage and the sort of trust in God that David had.

Father, help us to trust you with our problems, however big, however small, knowing that you are always ready to listen.

Extract from Slower than Butterflies, *first published* 1997.

David and Goliath

Junk box Jesus

❖

"I have come that they may have life, and have it to the full."
John 10:10

The other day I found Jesus in a junk box.

It happened at an antique fair. Under one dealer's table there was a cardboard box full of odds and ends. It was labelled 'Anything here £3.' I looked through it. Most of it was junk. There were odd plates from old tea sets, bits of brass, cheap prints in battered frames, and a few damp-stained copies of old novels.

Summer Market

And among them all, Jesus. A silvery image of him anyway, nailed to a cheap black wooden cross. A crucifix. I picked it up. For a moment I thought of buying it to rescue him from among all the junk in the cardboard box. I could take him home and put him somewhere more suitable, more respectable. Maybe on the wall in my studio.

Then something told me he wouldn't want to be rescued. He'd rather be there, where he was, in the junk box among the least-valued, the throw-away pieces from a throw-away society. Jesus always had time for throw-aways, the down-and-outs and the undervalued.

So I quietly put him back in the box and, as I did so, he seemed to nod and smile. Or was that just my imagination?

Lord of old and new,
open my eyes to your presence in everyone I see today.

Extract from Love is a Wild Bird, *first published* 2003.

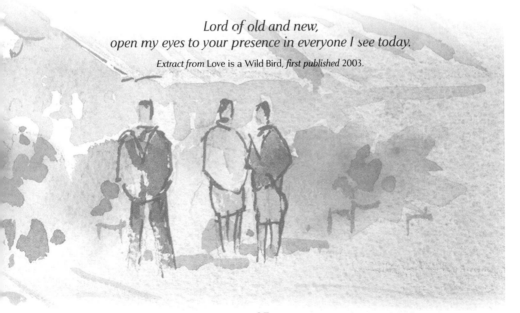

27

Awesome intelligence

"What is mankind that you are mindful of them,
a son of man that you care for him?
You made them a little lower than the angels;
you crowned them with glory and honour
and put everything under their feet."
Hebrews 2:6–8

We've been watching our sugar intake recently – hope our GP's listening. We're using a sugar substitute instead. It comes in those neat little green-and-white containers. Hold one over the cup, press the green top, and a tiny white tablet falls in. But the other day when I pressed it, nothing happened. It was empty. I shook it to make sure then, without thinking, I dumped it in the rubbish bin.

A moment later, I said to myself, "I wonder how it works?" I retrieved it. It took a bit of probing to find out how to open it up, but I managed it. And what a surprise. Only four components and that included just one moving part. A little thing we all take for granted, using it without thinking, and dumping it when it's empty. I'm no engineer, but to me the design was amazing – a cylinder, a base, a top and a little lever. So intricate, but so simple. The intelligence of the men or women who'd designed it was breathtaking.

And if that's amazing, take it one step back and think about the intelligence of the power who created men and women with the capacity to design such things for themselves. The intelligence many of us call God.

Lord of the imagination,
I'm breathless at the wonder of the world you created,
and all the people in it.
May I never undervalue it or them.

Extract from Dabbling with Ducks, *first published* 2007.

Snowed up, Derbyshire

Finding the natural rhythm

"Come to me, all you who are weary and burdened, and I will give you rest.
Take my yoke upon you and learn from me, for I am gentle and humble in heart,
and you will find rest for your souls.
For my yoke is easy and my burden is light."
Matthew 11:28–30

A Corner of the Woods

Walking around the garden the other morning between rain showers I saw something move in the long grass. Rather too much grass about, at the moment. It was a hedgehog, looking a bit miserable in the damp. I watched him for a bit until I realised he was watching me.

"Good morning, hedgehog," I said. "Funny sort of life you lead. Just rooting around in the hedge all day, looking for food. Don't you get bored? Not much of a diet either, is it? Just worms, slugs and insects. I don't think I'd like to be a hedgehog."

The hedgehog thought for a minute. Then he said, "I know what you mean, but look at it from my point of view. When autumn comes, I'll find a nice quiet hole somewhere, snuggle up warm and go to sleep right through the winter. You'll be out there working, shovelling snow and fending off double-glazing salesmen."

It is true. Nature has its seasons. Times of intense activity when every waking hour is busy. Finding food, growing, bringing up young. Then comes a time of rest, when everything winds down, seems to relax.

The trouble is that we humans have lost this natural rhythm. We rush around the whole time because that's what life seems to demand of us. And then we wonder why we crack up. We're human because that's the way God made us, and he knows that we can only do so much before we need a break. Relax.

Lord, slow me down.

Extract from Talking with Hedgehogs, *first published* 2001.

Relax and recharge

There is a time for everything, and a season for every activity under the heaven.
Ecclesiastes 3:1

A man who had worked hard all his life was asked what he would do in retirement. "For the first month," he said, "I'll sit on the porch in my rocking chair."

"And then what?" "Then I'll start rocking – slowly," he answered.

Why do we find it so hard to slow down? Most of us aren't human beings any more, we're human doings. We rush around madly from one thing to the next. Achievement is all that counts. We show each other full diaries, shake our heads and say we wish we had more spare time, but secretly we enjoy the thought that the world can't get along without us. That if we didn't do things, the earth would grind to a halt. That we are indispensable.

But this constant activity leaves us little time to look at who we are or where we're going. No time to think. A wise writer in the Bible said that there's a time for everything under the sun – and I reckon that includes a time to release ourselves, let go and recharge our batteries.

"Be still and know that I am God," the Psalmist advises. It means 'relax and know...'. The problem with our frenetic activity is that it crowds God out. We think our busy-ness is on his behalf, but really it pushes him to the edge of our lives. Take time out today, relax and give God a chance to make himself felt.

Lord, when life is fast and I am
getting breathless,
help me to feel your presence
in the pressures.

Extract from Talking with Hedgehogs,
first published 2001.

A Walk through the Woods

33

Taming the tongue

… but set an example for the believers in speech, in conduct,
in love, in faith and in purity.
1 Timothy 4:12

The box said 'Extra-thick baby wipes'. "Strange," I thought, "I've never seen any extra-thick babies. Chubby ones, yes, and not so chubby, but extra-thick babies? I'm surprised parents don't complain." Then there's 'Baby Changing Facilities'. I remember having thoughts like that when our kids were six months old and crying at three in the morning, but on the whole I guess parents are satisfied with the babies they've got and wouldn't want to change them.

And on the radio the other day a presenter described a man who "...was on crutches following an operation." I wondered where he was following the operation to? And wouldn't he have followed it better without the crutches?

It's so easy to say the wrong thing, put a double meaning where we hadn't intended to. Sometimes it's funny, but not always. It's easy to misunderstand what people say and to hear in their words meanings they never intended. And however hard we try people can misinterpret our words. And once the words are out we can't call them back.

The tongue is a bit of a problem isn't it? It's only a small part of the body but no-one has been able to tame it. It's not really the tongue – it's the mind.

So let's think before we speak, and when we speak, say it with love. And when we hear someone say something we don't like, give the other person a chance to explain before we sound off.

Summer Sunshine

The Chinese have a saying – don't they always? 'If you want to appear wise, don't open your mouth.' Maybe that goes for me, too.

Listening Lord, may I speak less and listen more today.
And in the listening may I hear the words that aren't said.

Extract from Talking with Hedgehogs, *first published* 2001.

Never let a problem fester

First go and be reconciled to them; then come and offer your gift.
Matthew 5:24

It's the little things that matter, says the proverb. Yes, and small things can grow and get out of proportion if we don't deal with them. A recent report said that thousands of lampposts across the country are weak and need replacing. The reason? Dogs. Male dogs to be specific.

Yes, you've guessed it. Apparently, when male dogs lift their legs to mark their territory, the acid in what they leave on the lamppost begins to corrode both the concrete and the iron reinforcing rods. In time, and many dogs later, the posts weaken and eventually become a danger. Female dogs, like our Milli, are much better behaved.

So small things do matter, but it's so easy to put them off. We don't want to face the person we had a disagreement with, or write the letter we ought to write but are struggling to find the right words. The bigger the problem grows, and the longer we leave it, the harder it gets to put right.

Our worries may not bring lampposts down, but it's better to face things, not by using acid comments, but by making a real attempt to get back on track with the one we've disagreed with. And there's no time like today to make a start.

Lord of paradox, remind me that I can only be right with my neighbour when I'm right with you, and only right with you when I'm right with my neighbour.

Extract from Dabbling with Ducks, *first published* 2007.

Milli and Ancient Oak

An open doorway

❖

"Ask and it will be given to you; seek and you will find; knock and the door will be opened to you."
Matthew 7:7

Farm Cottage, Norway

DIY – Do It Yourself. A friend once said that when he retired he'd make a fortune running a combined DIY and First Aid course. He reckoned that most people taking up carpentry or laying floor tiles end up cut or bruised. It's true – I have the scars to prove it.

I was hanging a door the other day and it was obeying Askew's DIY Law No. 2 which states that 'Every job takes twice as long as you think it will.' Incidentally, Askew's DIY Law No. 1 says, 'Every job is twice as complicated as you think it will be.' I've also discovered Law No. 3, which states that when you're holding up a door with one hand the screwdriver is just out of reach. The answer to all these laws is to pay someone else to do the job.

But I began to think about doors and what they're for. Are they to keep people out or to let people through? I suppose a bit of both really, but I think the letting through is the most important. If we simply wanted to keep people out, there would be no need for a door at all. Just block up the hole.

A door lets people in to share our space and allows us to get out into a wider world. Do you let people into your life, or do you keep the door firmly shut? Jesus talked about being a door, a door to new life. An opening to richer experience. And thinking about that someone said, "When you open the door of your life to God, you find he's already opened the door of his life to you."

Lord, may I find the courage to open the door of my life to you and to throw away the key.

Extract from Talking with Hedgehogs, *first published* 2001.

Trees with character

❖

That person is like a tree planted by streams of water, which yields its fruit in season and whose leaf does not wither.
Psalm 1:3

Trees have personalities. They're individuals. Tall or bushy, thick or thin, well-established or struggling, they're like people, each with its own character. Sometimes, as I walk around, I look at people and try to work out what sort of tree they are. Just for fun of course.

There are the old oaks. Folk who've gone through all the seasons, seen it all. They're often battle-scarred by life's winds but they're strong, they've survived. Then there are the beech trees. Smooth and elegant people, who grow more graceful the older they get. And what about the Scots pines? A bit dry and sombre, strong characters who take life seriously and with a whiff of self-denial about them. The willows and silver birches? Softer, more gentle, beautiful and feminine – but I won't let my imagination run away too far. Horse chestnuts? Dependable, fertile, generously offering their conkers every year.

Then there are saplings of all sorts. They're the young; adaptable and full of promise. The people who grow saplings used to be called nurserymen – a much more personal word than garden centre, isn't it? And the first Psalm in the Bible describes people who live well as 'trees planted by streams of water, healthy and full of life'. It also says they're fruitful. Think about it.

And no, I don't talk to trees. Not yet.

Lord, strengthen my roots in the soil of your love.

Extract from Love is a Wild Bird, *first published* 2003.

Facing the unknown

"Therefore I tell you, do not worry about your life, what you will eat or drink; or about your body, what you will wear. Is not life more than food, and the body more than clothes?"
Matthew 6:25

The Open Gate

At a conference in Denmark, I talked to a friend who had worked in a remote area of south-east Asia. He told me about someone who had taken a village worker into the city for the first time. They walked into a tall office block and needed to go to the sixth floor. There was the lift. Without thinking the man pressed the button, the lift came down and the door slid open. The villager stepped back in surprise. "What sort of room is this?" he asked, looking at the little metal box in front of him.

As my friend's colleague tried to explain, another man walked past, got into the lift and pressed the button. The door closed and the lift went up. They watched the indicator showing which floor the lift had reached: one, two, three, four. "See, it's all right," he said. "It's gone up and in a moment it'll come down again."

The lift came down. The door opened and out stepped a woman. The villager stared. "There's no way I'm going in there," he said, "if that's what happens." And he headed for the stairs.

No, I'm not sure if it ever really took place but it illustrates a point. What we don't know can be frightening. What we don't understand can be threatening. We worry and it doesn't help much when folk tell you not to. "Who says worry doesn't work?" said a man. "The things I worry about never seem to happen!"

You don't know what you're going to encounter today, but the chances are that you'll be able to cope with it. But if you can't, try sharing it with someone else. And if you're really stuck, try God – he's around all the time.

Today is unknown territory.
Whatever it may bring, Lord of the way, stay near.

Extract from Talking with Hedgehogs, *first published* 2001.

Finding inner calm

Accept one another, then, just as Christ accepted you…
Romans 15:7

Some people read the newspaper in the loo. That's easier with a tabloid than a broadsheet. But the other day a little book appeared on the windowsill in there. It was called *The Little Book of Calm* and the great thing about the book is that each page holds just one thought, a couple of sentences that you can read quickly and take to heart.

I say 'take to heart' – some of them you can take with a pinch of salt, like the one that says, 'Wear comfortable shoes'. A good idea, but not at the top of my list when it comes to measures to calm me down. 'Breathe less' is another. Slowing your breathing can help to calm you, but don't try to cut it out altogether. That would certainly calm you down but you wouldn't really feel the benefit.

Others are more helpful. 'Pretend to be human. Leave it to others to be perfect.' Now that's good advice. We try so hard to live up to other people's expectations, and our own. We try to be supermen and superwomen. Super cooks and super parents. We try to do everything perfectly. But it's not necessary. Now don't get me wrong. It's great to try to do the best we can but don't strive for the impossible. We're only human and that means none of us is perfect.

However hard we may try, we'll never be Nelson Mandela or Mother Teresa, Tom Cruise or Nicole Kidman. Just be happy to be you. Accept yourself as you are, that's the way Jesus accepts you, and then maybe a little calm will come into your life today.

Lord, you take my breath away. It's good to know that I'm accepted as I am.
Teach me to open my arms to others as wide as yours are to me.

Extract from Love *is a Wild Bird, first published* 2003.

Do not disturb!

❖

Then he returned to his disciples and found them sleeping...
Mark 14:37

I was on a long-haul flight to Singapore. Among the papers in the pocket of the seat in front of me was a bit of coloured card. On it, in large bright letters, it said, 'Do not disturb'.

When you want to sleep you put your seat into its recline position, sometimes to the annoyance of the person behind, display the notice and close your eyes. It's supposed to prevent interruptions. It doesn't always work, particularly if you are in an aisle seat and someone wants to get past you to go to the loo.

I thought it would be great if I could carry the notice around all the time, wherever I was. 'Do not disturb.' Bad news? Problems in the Middle East? Someone needing my help? 'Do not Disturb.' Just let me roll over and sleep. But it wouldn't work and I don't believe it should.

We need to be disturbed at times, to be jolted out of our comfortable ruts – by injustice, by suffering – and we have no inborn right to an easy life. And if we're disturbed enough by what goes on around us, we might just start doing something to help.

One last thing. If we did manage to sleep through the problems, we might miss the joys of life as well. I wouldn't want to do that. Would you?

A Quiet Afternoon at the Lake

Lord, life with you can be uncomfortable.
Keep me awake, the excitement makes it all worthwhile.

Extract from Love is a Wild Bird, *first published* 2003.

Daily love

Love is patient, love is kind. It does not envy, it does not boast,
it is not proud. It does not dishonour others, it is not self-seeking,
it is not easily angered, it keeps no record of wrongs.
Love does not delight in evil but rejoices with the truth.
It always protects, always trusts, always hopes, always perseveres.
1 Corinthians 13:4–7

When we moved house we had to find a new plumber. It wasn't easy getting one, but when Jim turned up he was very helpful. He's a competent, conscientious and cheerful worker, and a conversationalist.

He told us a lot about his family. There's a teenage son, tragically hit by multiple sclerosis, and a wife Jim obviously adores. "She's a great woman, my wife," he said, "and we've got a good marriage. In 30 years she's never run out of coffee or toilet paper." We laughed.

There are many ways of showing love. The glossy magazines say diamonds are best. The slightly more modest weeklies advise us to say it with flowers. A hug, a kiss, a held hand, all help.

And there's the coffee and toilet paper way. I'm not suggesting this is women's work, but the faithful, quiet work that keeps homes going, keeps relationships good. The attention to detail, making sure that the everyday things are cared for. It may be earthy, but it's no less valuable for that.

The cup of coffee, and the rest, speak for themselves. Speak of looking ahead, anticipating needs, meeting them with loving ordinariness.

"Love is patient; love is kind..." writes Paul to Christians at Corinth, "Love will never come to an end." And whether we write books about it, or express it simply through the weekly shopping list, it all has meaning. Love expressed in an infinity of ways, mostly quiet.

Love is still at the centre of the universe. Still available. And God, who is love, is still trying to pour it into our lives.

So many ways, Lord, in which you show your love.
Sometimes, its very ordinariness surprises me.
No drama here, no lightning flash or thunder-clap.
Just faithfulness, in spite of all I do to make it difficult.
I make myself unlovely, yet still your love surrounds me,
seeks out the cracks in the hard shell of my ego,
and seeps in unrecognised.

Extract from Facing the Storm, *first published* 1989.

A Splash of Colour

The benefits of chocolate

A news item on the radio grabbed my attention. "Chocolate," it said, "is good for you." Wow!

Later I followed it up on the internet. Who wouldn't, hearing those words? And it seemed to be true. Chocolate, I'm told, contains chemicals that may help prevent cancer and heart disease. But before we all rush out and form a queue outside the local corner shop, let's look at the small print.

The research was financed by a well-known chocolate-making company and there were only 40 people in the test. You also need to eat an awful lot of chocolate before it has any real effect and that amount of sugar might not be good for you anyway. It also claimed that eating chocolate in moderation – now that's a contradiction in terms – can help us live longer. I wonder.

Today, it might help if the people in the Third World who grow the cocoa beans were paid enough to give them a healthy lifestyle. So, when you hear reports like these, I suggest you do as the Bible says, and be as wise as serpents and harmless as doves. Thank the Lord for chocolate and leave it at that.

Although, if they need people for more research on the benefits of chocolate, count me in.

In the Tall Grass

Lord, my blessings come from you.
Remind me that they taste better when they're shared.

Extract from Love is a Wild Bird, *first published* 2003.

Making prayer a priority

Be joyful in hope, patient in affliction, faithful in prayer.
Romans 12:12

A doctor friend of mine told me about a patient who phoned early one morning. "Please can I come to see you? It's urgent." My friend's appointment list was full, but he told the man to come anyway, promising to fit him in as soon as he could. The man came and sat in the waiting room. After some time, the doctor called for him. "Sorry," said the receptionist. "He's gone. He said he couldn't wait any longer or he'd miss his prayer time. He said he'd come back later."

The patient returned, later in the day. He told the doctor. "I had a very painful abscess, but I had to go and pray. And," he added, "after I'd prayed, the abscess burst. I'm already feeling much better."

Talking to me later, my friend said, "Perhaps his prayer was more effective than my medical treatment would've been!" At least the man had a clear idea of his priorities, and put prayer higher up the list than his personal comfort or convenience.

There's a thought for all of us.

And it was only at the end of the conversation that my friend added, "Oh yes, one other thing... my patient was a Muslim."

Lord, help me hold prayer as dear as he,
and leave the judgement where it most belongs.
With you.

Extract from Breaking the Rules, *first published* 1992.

Evening Shadows

The wonder of creation

How many are your works, LORD!
In wisdom you made them all; the earth is full of your creatures.
Psalm 104:24

I went to the vet the other day. Not for myself – I'm not quite as disillusioned with the National Health Service as that – I took one of our dogs. While I was waiting I picked up a leaflet – 'Caring for Elderly Dogs'.

The leaflet began by describing old dogs and the more I read the more it sounded like me. 'Greying round the muzzle' – yes, that's me. 'Changes in body shape' – I'm afraid so. 'Stiffness in the joints' – certainly in my knees. 'Reluctance to take exercise' – yes, I admit it. 'Bladder problems'... I'll stop right there otherwise it might get a bit personal. And I know people say that dog owners get to look like their pets but that's taking it a bit far.

It made me think though. The similarities remind me that we humans are as much part of God's creation as anything else and, if we realised that, we might begin to treat the earth and other living things a bit differently.

Of course we are different from animals in some ways – in being able to talk, to think, to imagine. And in our feelings for the spiritual. To wonder what life is about, and to realise there's more to it than just what we can see and measure. And that more is God, who created you and me, and my dogs, and wants the best for all of us.

And if we can begin to take that into account we may find it easier to live in harmony with each other, the world about us, and with the God who made us.

Extract from Slower than Butterflies, *first published* 1997.

Lord God, Creator, all life is yours.
All that has come to be has come through you.
Lives in your energy, takes breath because you willed it.
Is clothed in your beauty, your dignity.
Part of your world. Valued and loved.

Extract from Many Voices One Voice, *first published 1985.*

A D ASKEW

Milli, Waiting to Pounce

In God's hands...

❖

But I trust in you, LORD;
I say, 'You are my God.' My times are in your hands...
Psalm 31:14–15

Watching our youngest granddaughter tying her shoelaces, I marvel at how quickly children learn. Tying laces is a pretty complicated thing to do. There's a website on the internet which proves that. It's called *Ian's Shoelace Site.*

The author, Ian, has analysed the way we tie shoelace knots. He reckons there are at least 15 different ways of doing it, although most of us use the same one all the way through life.

But Ian goes further. He's invented his own knot and claims it's the fastest ever for tying shoelaces securely. Now I'm full of admiration for people with enquiring minds

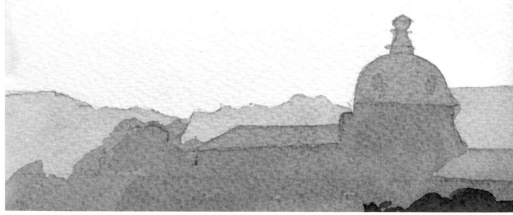

Prague Sunset

56

but I do question whether saving one and a half seconds a day is a major contribution to human civilisation. I calculate that I'd need to tie my shoelaces 70 times to cover the time this *Thought for the Day* takes to read, or 400 times to save ten minutes.

We seem obsessed by time, yet the important thing isn't about trying to save a frantic second here or there but using the time we have positively. And we forget that all of it, my time and yours, is in God's hands anyway.

Lord of time and eternity, I don't know what today may bring,
but I know you're just around the corner. Thank you.

Extract from Dabbling with Ducks, *first published* 2007.

More than a number

"The one who enters by the gate is the shepherd of the sheep. The gatekeeper opens the gate for him, and the sheep listen to his voice. He calls his own sheep by name and leads them out."
John 10:2–3

Walking through the city centre I saw women with clipboards, pens poised. With bright smiles they were approaching shoppers. "Just five minutes, madam, to ask you a few questions. I hope you can spare the time."

The questions they ask are wide. What newspaper do you read? Which deodorant do you use? How much chocolate do you buy each week? How much do you believe what politicians say on a scale of 1 to 10?

Sometimes I try to side-step them but I must admit they rarely stop me anyway. Even though I've no desire to share my preference in wholemeal bread with a stranger, I must admit I sometimes feel a bit left out. Ignored. Why don't they stop me? Isn't my opinion valuable?

But when they do stop me they usually make it quite clear that the whole exercise is anonymous. They don't want my name or address. They're not interested in me as a person, not even as a name. I'm just another filled-in form to be added to all the other filled-in forms, to be fed into a computer, chewed and digested, the results tabulated and put onto a marketing manager's desk. For lunch.

Jesus describes himself as a shepherd who knows his sheep so well that he calls each of them by name. We're not just numbers to God, we're individuals, valued for what we are, not just for the bits of information we can offer to some celestial computer. Every hair on our head is numbered; our personalities respected. And we're loved infinitely by an infinite God.

And, in the same passage from the gospel, Jesus the shepherd offers us not an improved brand of cornflakes but new life.

Extract from Slower than Butterflies, *first published* 1997.

Lord, I'm overwhelmed. It's just too much for me to understand.
Why you, creator of the galaxies, the power that spins the planets,
weaves the stars into your tapestry of love can still have time for me.
I would have thought the universe would be enough for you.

Extract from Encounters, *first published* 1997.

Market in Voss

Positive appreciation

Therefore encourage one another and build each other up,
just as in fact you are doing.
1 Thessalonians 5:11

End of term, and it's time for school reports. Thankfully, I'm way past that, and our daughters are well past it too. So now it's the grandchildren's turn. Georgia – yes, you've heard of her before – is eight years old now and is a very upfront character. Very different from her elder sister, Claudia, who has an equally enquiring mind but is happiest curled up with a book way beyond her reading age.

Their school reports were both very good and encouraging, their mum told me on the phone, but one little comment caught our attention. Her class teacher had written, 'Georgia is orally enthusiastic.' Well, that's a nice way of saying that Georgia talks a lot – a fact we can confirm from personal experience – but I enjoyed the appreciative feel of the words her teacher used. From being a criticism, as it might have been, the teacher had turned it into a more positive comment, with a bit of humour.

I wish all criticism and observation of our lives and characters could be made in that sort of mould, and then maybe something good could come out of it. And there's no point in waiting for others to begin the process. We can start with ourselves. Whenever we have something to say, any observation about a friend, let's make it appreciative rather than critical.

An artist once said, "Nobody ever put up a statue to a critic."

Summer Conversation

*Encouraging Lord, teach me the quiet word, the helpful word,
the word that builds and strengthens those who hear.*

Extract from Dabbling with Ducks, *first published* 2007.

Lord,
teach me to dance
in the joy of your presence today.
And help me to reflect
the beauty of your world
in my life.

Norfolk Village